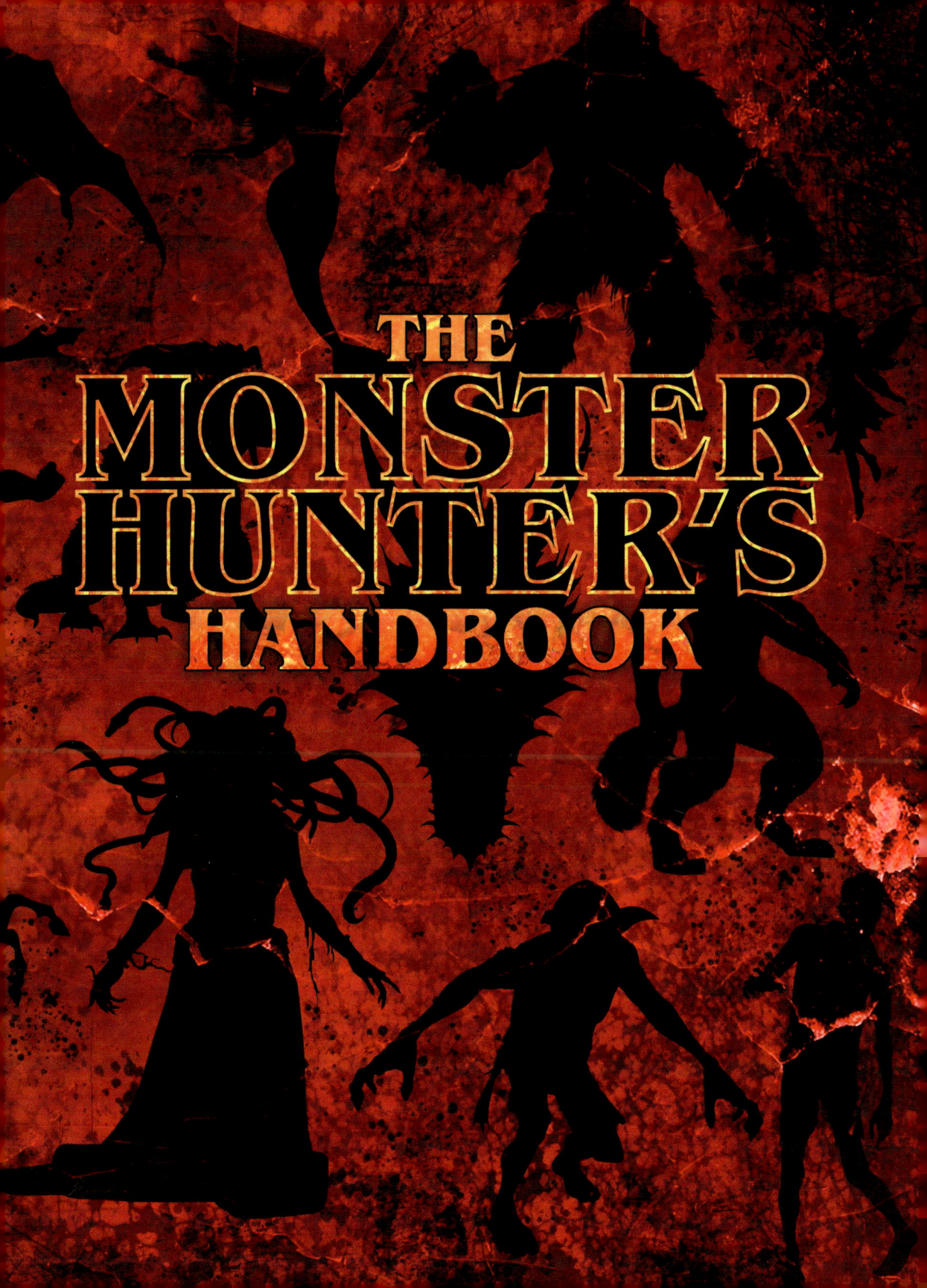

Published in the UK by Scholastic, 2024
1 London Bridge, London, SE1 9BG
Scholastic Ireland, 89E Lagan Road, Dublin Industrial Estate,
Glasnevin, Dublin, D11 HP5F

SCHOLASTIC and associated logos are trademarks and/or
registered trademarks of Scholastic Inc.

Text © Scholastic, 2024
Designed by Grant Kempster for Cloud King Creative
Illustrations by Grant Kempster, iStock.com and
Shutterstock.com

ISBN 978 0702 33121 3

A CIP catalogue record for this book is available from
the British Library.

All rights reserved.
This book is sold subject to the condition that it shall not,
by way of trade or otherwise, be lent, hired out or otherwise
circulated in any form of binding or cover other than that
in which it is published. No part of this publication may be
reproduced, stored in a retrieval system, or transmitted in
any form or by any other means (electronic, mechanical,
photocopying, recording or otherwise) without prior written
permission of Scholastic Limited.

Printed and bound in China
Paper made from wood grown in sustainable forests
and other controlled sources.

1 3 5 7 9 10 8 6 4 2

www.scholastic.co.uk

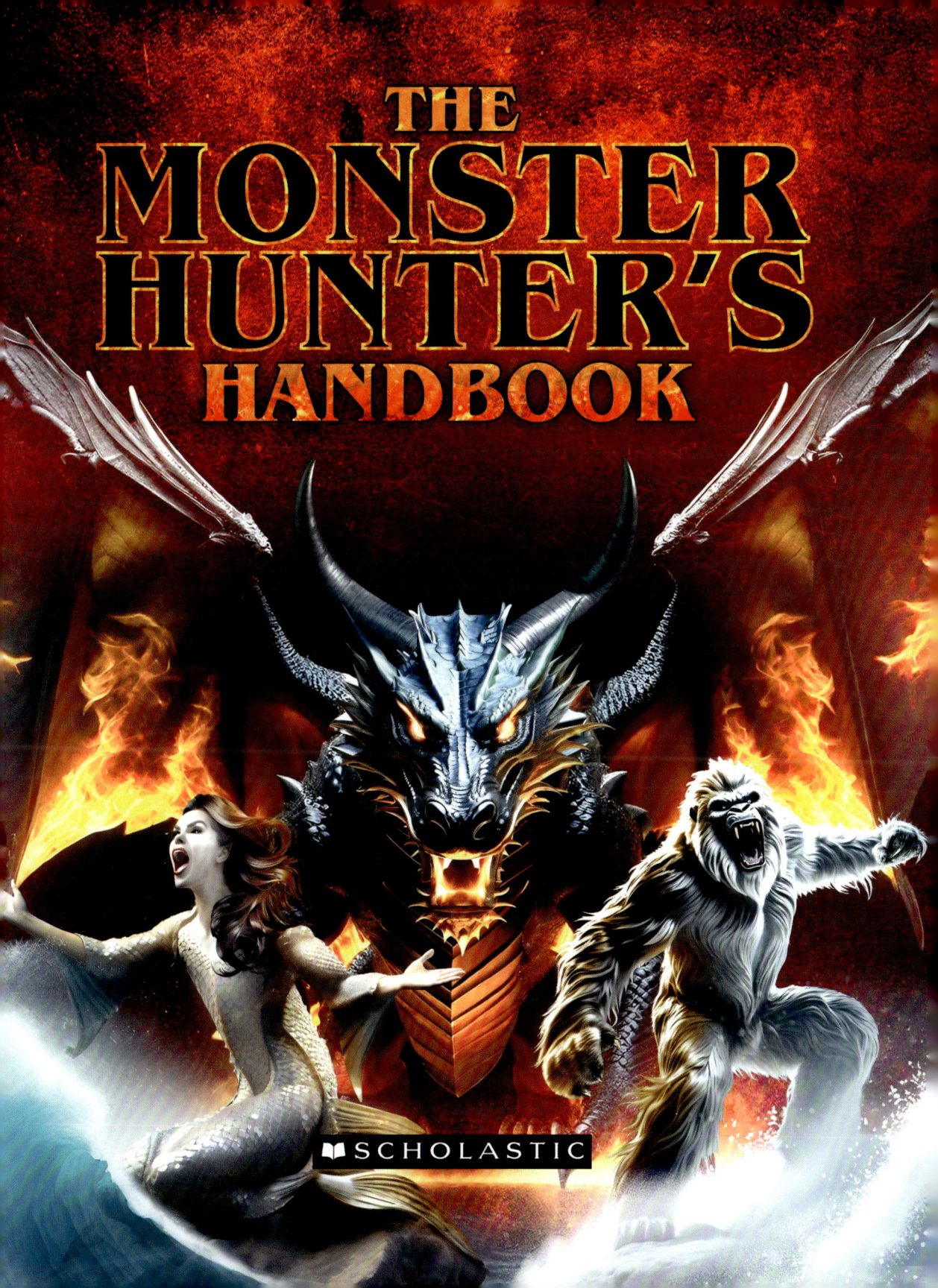

CONTENTS

Basilisks 10
Myth Busting 12
Bunyips. 14
A Deadly Dog 16
The Chimera 18
Make a Warrior's Shield. 20
Cyclopes 22
Recipe: Monster Cookies 24
Dragons 26
Create a Creature 28
Fauns 30
Monster Mash 32
Fairies 34
Join the Hunt! 36
Goblins 38
How to Draw a Griffin 40
Gorgons 42
Monster Discovery 44
The Kraken 46
Potion-Making 48

The Loch Ness Monster 50
Nightmare! 52
Mermaids 54
Quiz: Would You Rather? 56
The Minotaur 58
Spooky Celebrations 60
Ogres 62
Fright Night 64
Phoenixes 66
Monster Moves 68
Unicorns 70
Ghouls Gallery 72
Vampires 74
How to Avoid a Vampire Encounter 76
Werewolves 78
Fact or Folklore? 80
The Yeti 82
In Search of Monsters 84
Zombies 86
How to Survive a Zombie Apocalypse . . . 88
Quiz: Which Mythical Monster Are You? 90
Answers 92

INTRODUCTION

Fearsome beasts have featured in stories since ancient times, their battles with human heroes legendary. From the bloodthirsty basilisk to cursed zombies, these creatures possessing epic strength or even supernatural powers have always fascinated and terrified us.

Today, more mysterious mythical monsters continue to be 'uncovered' around the world, with strange sightings of unidentified creatures reported in every continent. Turn the pages to meet some of the world's most fantastical creatures – learn about their origins, their extraordinary abilities and woeful weaknesses, then decide which beasts you dare track down on an epic adventure like never before.

Monsters are out there . . . now go and find them!

BASILISKS

Much mystery surrounds the mythical basilisk, versions of which include a **huge reptile**, a giant serpent and a half-rooster half-lizard creature. Feared for its **deathly stare** and the venomous trail it leaves in its wake, the basilisk is among the most **dangerous** of beasts.

APPEARANCE: a slithering serpent-reptile, some say the basilisk had legs, while others describe its leathery wings

ORIGIN: Europe – ancient Greece and Rome

ALSO KNOWN AS: King of Serpents, cockatrice

STRENGTHS: a deadly gaze, a venomous bite, fire-breathing, flight (the cockatrice)

WEAKNESSES: weasels – they can withstand the basilisk's glare and are immune to its venom

DANGER RATING:
💀💀💀💀

A staring contest with this creature is likely to end badly!

FIVE THINGS YOU SHOULD KNOW ABOUT BASILISKS

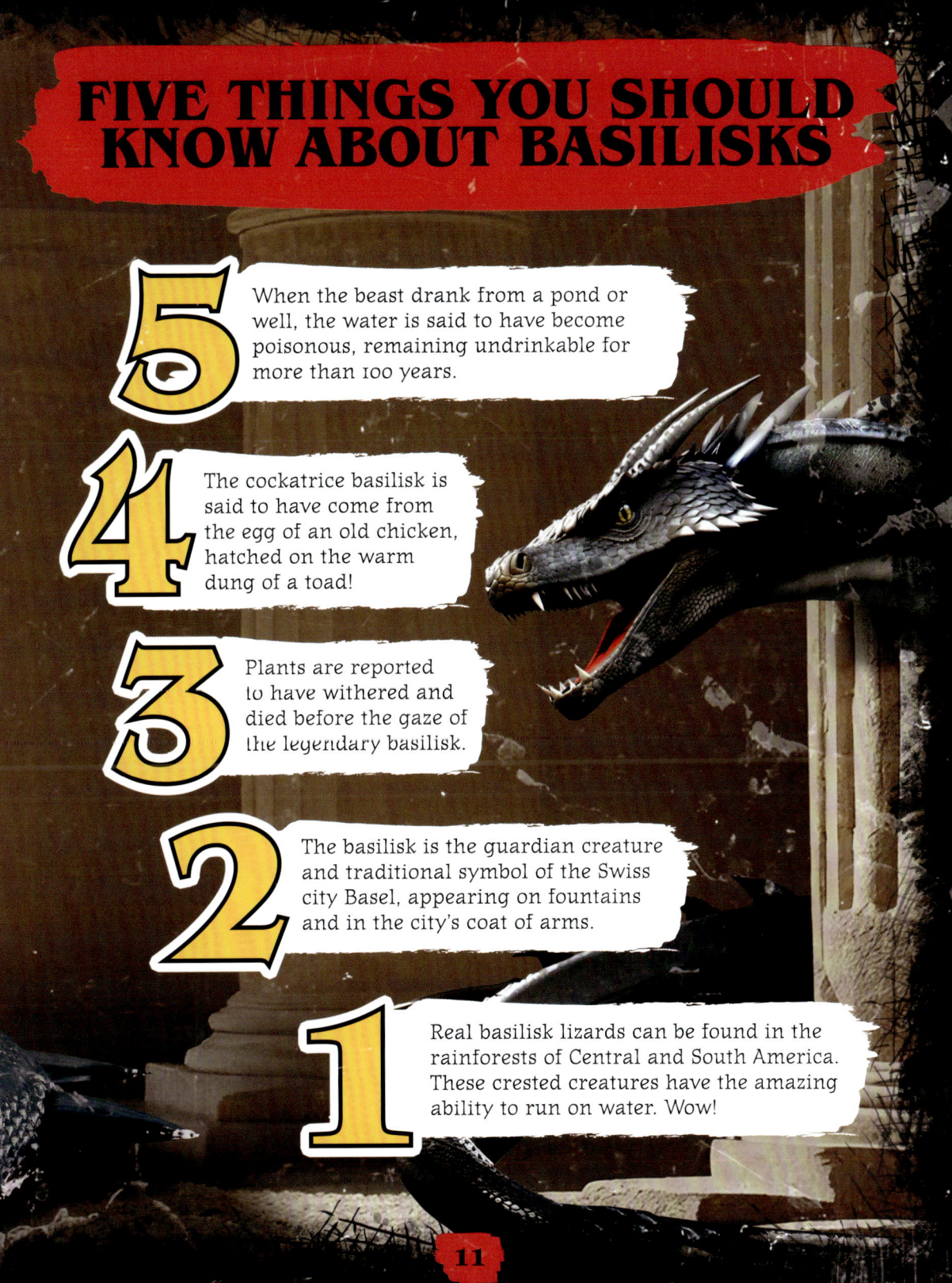

5 When the beast drank from a pond or well, the water is said to have become poisonous, remaining undrinkable for more than 100 years.

4 The cockatrice basilisk is said to have come from the egg of an old chicken, hatched on the warm dung of a toad!

3 Plants are reported to have withered and died before the gaze of the legendary basilisk.

2 The basilisk is the guardian creature and traditional symbol of the Swiss city Basel, appearing on fountains and in the city's coat of arms.

1 Real basilisk lizards can be found in the rainforests of Central and South America. These crested creatures have the amazing ability to run on water. Wow!

MYTH BUSTING

Only Odysseus was able to solve the Sphinx's riddle, a creature with the body of a lion and a human head. Try to solve her tricky teaser, then work out which mythological monsters are describing themselves in the riddles that follow.

I walk on four legs in the morning, two legs at noon and three legs at night. What am I?
Answer:

1 I may have wings, but I'm not a bird, And while I lay eggs I'm neither feathered nor furred. What am I?
Answer:

2 Don't come too close or you may burn, When one life ends I soon return. What am I?
Answer:

3 I don't need to eat, but have a gruesome thirst, I emerge at night, but sleep all day first. What am I?
Answer:

4 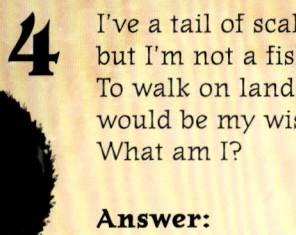 I've a tail of scales, but I'm not a fish To walk on land would be my wish. What am I?

Answer:

5  I've plenty of hair that's no good for wool, Watch me put in a shift when the moon is full. What am I?

Answer:

6  I once was human, but can no longer talk, I may look like death, yet I'm able to walk. What am I?

Answer:

7 Neither bull nor goat There's a horn on my head, Used not to attack, but to heal instead. What am I?

Answer:

8  A watery monster I stay out of sight, Yet some claim they've seen me – do you think they're right? What am I?

Answer:

BUNYIPS

With dark shaggy fur, the bunyip shares similarities with both dogs and seals. Aboriginal legends tell of the creature dwelling in the swamps and waterholes of Australia, where it lures **human prey** into the murky waters.

- **APPEARANCE:** dark fur, often disguised by mud and swamp weeds, teeth like a hippopotamus, walrus-like tusks

- **ORIGIN:** Australia and Tasmania

- **ALSO KNOWN AS:** kianpraty, wowee and more – its name usually translates as 'evil spirit'

- **STRENGTHS:** can breathe underwater for long periods, a powerful bite, speedy swimmer

- **WEAKNESSES:** this amphibious beast can't stray far from water

DANGER RATING: 💀💀💀
Beware of the bunyip!

FIVE THINGS YOU SHOULD KNOW ABOUT BUNYIPS

5 The screech of a bunyip was more likely the cry of a seal or bittern marsh bird in reality.

4 Although the bunyip possesses long claws and sharp teeth, it prefers to deliver a deadly hug to overpower its prey.

3 Bunyips have incredible vision, and are able to see in great detail, both in complete darkness and underwater.

2 Despite its scare factor, this species is said to be shy. Young bunyips tend to stick with their parents until they are fully grown.

1 Early accounts of the bunyip describe it having a single large eye.

A DEADLY DOG

Hades' triple-headed hellhound **Cerberus** helped guard the gates to the **underworld** in ancient Greece.

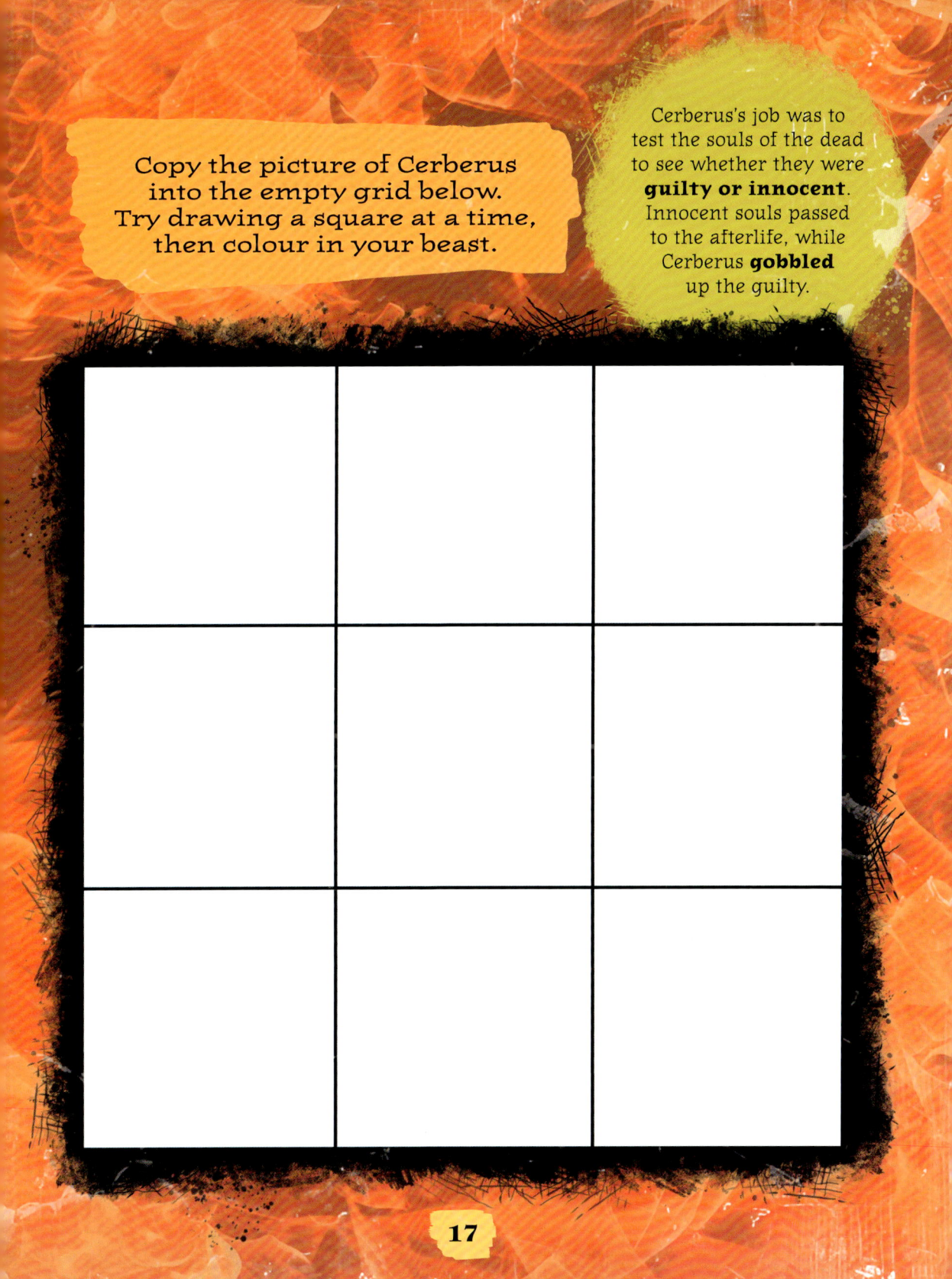

THE CHIMERA

Chimera is a beast from Greek mythology that was part lion, part goat and part snake. She was the daughter of the **fearsome monsters** Typhon and Echidna, the greatest adversaries to the **gods of Olympus**.

APPEARANCE: a lion's head and body with a second head of a goat and a serpent's tail

ORIGIN: ancient Lycia (modern-day Turkey)

ALSO KNOWN AS: Chimaera

STRENGTHS: fire-breathing, the power of a lion and a serpent's venom

WEAKNESSES: not immortal, fell to a surprise attack from behind

DANGER RATING: 💀💀💀
A horrible hybrid!

FIVE THINGS YOU SHOULD KNOW ABOUT THE CHIMERA

5 Fire-breathing Chimera terrorized the ancient kingdom of Lycia and was once thought to be invincible.

4 Chimera was believed to be responsible for natural disasters that were more likely due to volcanic eruptions in ancient Lycia.

3 She was slayed by Greek hero Bellerophon on the back of the winged horse Pegasus, who speared Chimera from behind.

2 After her death, Chimera joined Cerberus, gorgons and centaurs at the gates to the underworld alongside Hades.

1 The word 'chimera' is now used to mean a fantastical idea or figment of the imagination.

MAKE A WARRIOR'S SHIELD

If you're brave enough to battle some of the cruellest creatures in history, then you'll need all the help you can get! Craft a fine shield to help protect you against dragons, ogres and more!

You will need:
- a large cardboard box or strong cardboard
- marker pens
- scissors
- PVA glue
- acrylic paint
- paintbrushes

1 Draw a shield shape on the largest side panel of your cardboard box, then cut it out. It could be round, rectangular, oval or a traditional 'shield' shape.

Tip: to make your shield extra strong, cut out two identical shield shapes and stick them together.

2 Cut out two long rectangular card handles. One should be larger to make an armhole, while the other will be a handhold. Glue these in place on the back of the shield.

3 This next step is optional – either line the front of the shield with white paper or use papier-mâché to make a smooth painting surface.

4 When the shield has completely dried, paint a design of your choice on to the front. You might want to include a mythical monster to send your enemies running.

5 Leave to dry, then try on your new shield for size!

CYCLOPES

These **giant creatures** possessed enormous strength and a single eye in the middle of their forehead. Despite their fearsome appearance, most cyclopes were **helpful beasts**, willing to help the Olympian gods in battle.

APPEARANCE: one-eyed giants that stood between two and four metres tall

ORIGIN: ancient Greece

ALSO KNOWN AS: kyklops, 'round-eyes'

STRENGTHS: master builders, blacksmiths and shepherds

WEAKNESSES: some were thought to be not too bright

DANGER RATING:
 Giant, but gentle

FIVE THINGS YOU SHOULD KNOW ABOUT CYCLOPES

5 The original cyclopes in Greek mythology were the three brothers Brontes, Steropes and Arges, who together crafted Zeus's powerful thunderbolt.

4 The name 'cyclopes' meant 'circle-eyes' or 'round-eyes' from ancient Greek.

3 The walls of many ancient Greek cities were said to have been built by cyclopes.

2 Some stories state that cyclopes lived solitary lives, dwelling in caves or on mountain peaks.

1 A famous myth tells of the Greek warrior Odysseus the Cunning escaping death by blinding the cyclopes, Polyphemus.

MONSTER EYEBALL COOKIES

All your friends will be eyeing up these terrifying treats! They may look strange but they taste great. Try the recipe for yourself...

You will need:
- non-stick baking paper
- 150 g butter
- 75 g golden caster sugar
- 2 tsp vanilla extract
- 1 egg
- 300 g flour
- food colouring (optional)
- a packet of edible eyeballs or white chocolate chips and an edible cake pen

1 Ask an adult to pre-heat the oven to 180 °C (160 °C fan). Line two baking trays with non-stick baking paper.

Tip: ask an adult to help you when using the oven and microwave.

2 Cream the butter, sugar and vanilla extract together in a mixing bowl until smooth.

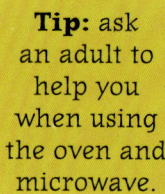

3 Add the egg and stir, then gradually add the flour, continuing to mix until you form a soft dough. If you want to add food colouring, add a few drops now, first splitting the dough for each colour.

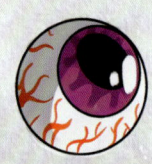

4 Wrap the dough or balls of dough in cling film and chill in the fridge for 30 minutes.

5 Roll out the dough until it is ½ cm thick on a board dusted with a little flour. Cut out circle shapes using a cutter or try this freehand.

6 Place on the baking trays and push a few eyeballs into each cookie. If you can't find these, try using white chocolate chips and decorate with your cake pen after cooking.

7 Bake for 10-12 minutes – the cookies should be a little soft. Ask an adult to remove the trays from the oven and leave to cool on a wire rack.

8 Share your snacks for a spooky treat – maybe even at a sleepover!

DRAGONS

Huge winged creatures, dragons have been feared for centuries in Europe, Asia and beyond. These serpent-like beasts were said to be able to breathe fire, spit venom and even shapeshift. While some dragons were tasked with guarding treasure, others were vicious predators.

APPEARANCE: serpent beasts with scaly skin, usually reported to have wings and a barbed tail

ORIGIN: Great Britain, Europe and Asia

ALSO KNOWN AS: drake, draco

STRENGTHS: expert fliers, can breathe fire, scaly armoured skin

WEAKNESSES: fire (surprisingly!), poison

DANGER RATING: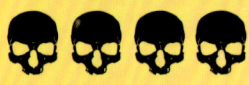

Lizard-like legends... with wings!

FIVE THINGS YOU SHOULD KNOW ABOUT DRAGONS

5 In Chinese culture, the dragon symbolizes good fortune, power and nobility. It is the fifth sign of the Chinese zodiac.

4 Discoveries of ancient dinosaur fossils in the Middle Ages led people to believe these were the bones of dragons.

3 The nations of Bhutan, Wales and Malta all display a dragon on their national flags.

2 'Dragons' can still be seen in the wild today – komodo dragons are giant lizards that can grow to over two and a half metres long.

1 The most famous dragon-slayer was St George, the patron saint of England and Catalonia, who freed the settlement of Silene (somewhere in modern-day Libya) from a venomous dragon.

CREATE A CREATURE

If you could design a mythical creature or bring one back from the dead, what would it look like and what would it be called? Choose from the following options, deciding whether your creation will be a beautiful beast or the stuff of nightmares.

Features:
- [ ] wings
- [ ] scales
- [ ] feathers
- [ ] fur
- [ ] smooth skin
- [ ] horns
- [ ] fins
- [ ] beak
- [ ] claws

other ideas:
....

How many?

	1	2	3+
heads	☐	☐	☐
eyes	☐	☐	☐
legs	☐	☐	☐
tails	☐	☐	☐
teeth	☐	☐	☐
wings	☐	☐	☐
horns	☐	☐	☐

How big?
- [ ] as tiny as a fairy
- [ ] lion-sized
- [ ] as huge as a dragon

other ideas:
....

Abilities:
- [ ] super strength
- [ ] fire-breathing
- [ ] shape-shifting
- [ ] healing powers
- [ ] magic
- [ ] deadly gaze
- [ ] expert flier

other ideas:
....

Where will it live?
- [ ] mountains
- [ ] forest
- [ ] ocean
- [ ] desert
- [ ] cave

other ideas:
....

Now draw your mythical monster and decide on an epic name.

Turn the page sideways if you need to.

FAUNS

Part-human, part-goat, fauns were spirit gods of the forest in Roman times. They descended from the leader of the fauns, the god Faunus and the goddess Fauna. Fearful travellers were said to encounter fauns in faraway, wild places, while other stories tell of kinder creatures helping those who were lost to find the right path.

APPEARANCE: a human upper body with the legs and horns of a goat. Unlike part-horse centaurs, fauns walked on two legs

ORIGIN: ancient Rome

ALSO KNOWN AS: Greek satyrs (but they are actually different creatures)

STRENGTHS: their wooden flutes could produce hypnotic melodies, while their goat legs deliver a strong kick

WEAKNESSES: their wild nature can lead them to trouble, often foolish

DANGER RATING:
☠ **Generally gentle creatures**

FIVE THINGS YOU SHOULD KNOW ABOUT FAUNS

5 They were later associated with the Greek god Pan, a panpipe-playing faun.

4 Some fauns possessed human feet instead of goat's hooves. A strange look!

3 The more charming among these creatures are party animals and love making music and merriment.

2 Mr Tumnus is perhaps the most famous fictional faun. He appears in *The Chronicles of Narnia* by C. S. Lewis.

1 Fauns were often portrayed as protectors of shepherds and their flocks.

MONSTER MASH

Can you identify each demon in this dreadful dozen? Study their silhouettes, then unscramble their names.

1 GROE

_ _ _ _

2 MAIMDER

_ _ _ _ _ _ _

3 BOMIZE

_ _ _ _ _ _

4 LEWFOREW

_ _ _ _ _ _ _ _

5 FRINGIF

_ _ _ _ _ _ _

6

ROGNAD
_ _ _ _ _ _

BLINGO
_ _ _ _ _ _

7

8

RENKAK
_ _ _ _ _ _

9

SLIKSIAB
_ _ _ _ _ _ _ _

10

MAVIERP
_ _ _ _ _ _ _

11

EITY
_ _ _ _

12

POXIHEN
_ _ _ _ _ _ _

FAIRIES

According to folklore, fairies were once considered to be **mischievous spirits** rather than wish-granting friends. Often known for their beauty, these tiny human-like creatures had **delicate wings** and often possessed **magical powers**.

APPEARANCE: often tiny winged creatures, they can grow to human size

ORIGIN: Europe

ALSO KNOWN AS: faeries, fae. Related to the fairy species are sprites, imps, pixies and brownies

STRENGTHS: flight, healing, can communicate with animals, shape-shifting, magic and even invisibility

WEAKNESSES: salt, iron and the herbs St John's Wort and yarrow

DANGER RATING:

Magical but mischievous

FIVE THINGS YOU SHOULD KNOW ABOUT FAIRIES

5 Centuries ago, many believed fairies to be the spirits of the dead.

4 They live longer lives than humans, but are not thought to be immortal.

3 In Irish folklore, a leprechaun is a small fairy or sprite who could be made to reveal the location of treasure if captured.

2 Fairies do not possess the ability to tell a lie, although they don't always tell the whole truth.

1 Rowan and hawthorn trees are considered sacred by fairies, to be protected at all costs.

JOIN THE HUNT!

If ghouls and goblins don't scare you, then monster hunting might just be the job for you! Before you get started, though, you're going to need a new name that sounds the business. Follow the instructions below to reveal it.

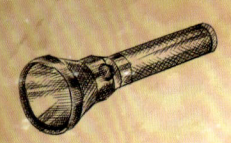

First, find the day on which you were born…

1st	– Fairy	17th	– Centaur
2nd	– Gnome	18th	– Zombie
3rd	– Yeti	19th	– Cerberus
4th	– Chimera	20th	– Kraken
5th	– Vampire	21st	– Demon
6th	– Sasquatch	22nd	– Oni
7th	– Loch Ness Monster	23rd	– Griffin
8th	– Bunyip	24th	– Siren
9th	– Werewolf	25th	– Unicorn
10th	– Hydra	26th	– Minotaur
11th	– Dragon	27th	– Faun
12th	– Cyclopes	28th	– Ghoul
13th	– Ogre	29th	– Phoenix
14th	– Mermaid	30th	– Wendigo
15th	– Basilisk	31st	– Gorgon
16th	– Troll		

Then look for the month in which you were born...

January — Buster
February — Catcher
March — Tracker
April — Hunter
May — Chaser
June — Trailer
July — Searcher
August — Doctor
September — Sleuth
October — Spotter
November — Breaker
December — Seeker

Write your monster hunter name here:

GOBLINS

Gruesome, green and **greedy for gold,** these creepy little creatures range from merely mischievous to much meaner – trust a goblin at **your own risk**. Goblins have been common in European folklore for centuries and now turn up in stories worldwide.

APPEARANCE: between just under a metre to a metre and a quarter tall, heads are usually large, greenish skin

ORIGIN: Europe, Asia and beyond

ALSO KNOWN AS: hobgoblin, imp, sprite

STRENGTHS: some goblins can perform basic magic, including making themselves invisible or changing shape

WEAKNESSES: their craving for gold often lands them in trouble

DANGER RATING: 💀💀
Tricky little fiends

FIVE THINGS YOU SHOULD KNOW ABOUT GOBLINS

5 Goblins historically lived in grottos, but these days prefer to hide in human households, causing havoc once darkness has fallen.

4 Goblins are skilled silversmiths and metal workers, able to forge fine weapons and armour.

3 Slyness is a common characteristic among goblins; they can in slip into shadows, avoiding detection.

2 Hobgoblins are the most mischievous kind of goblin; some are perilous pranksters, while others are cunning thieves.

1 Goblins love to sing, although their haunting melodies and strange lyrics are not always suitable for human ears!

HOW TO DRAW A GRIFFIN

With the head and wings of an **eagle** and the rear of a **lion**, has there ever been a mythical monster more majestic than the griffin? Follow these steps to draw your own **glorious griffin**.

You will need:
- a piece of paper
- a sharpened pencil
- a rubber
- coloured pens, pencils or crayons

1 Pressing lightly, draw a large oval for the griffin's body, a small oval for the head and a second small oval next to the body. (We'll rub out these shapes later on.)

2 Draw lines to join the shapes together, with small flicks on the griffin's neck.

DID YOU KNOW? According to legend, griffins fiercely guarded the gold and treasures of kings.

3 Add a feathered crest, a line at the front of its head and a beady eye.

4 Now add in the griffin's sharp, hooked beak.

5 Draw the two front legs next, using short, feathery strokes again.

6 Add the griffin's left foot next, with three talons at the front and one at the back. Its right leg should be partly hidden.

7 Now for the hind legs: the left leg appears longer, while the right leg is set back slightly. Add the lion-like rear feet with toes and the claws next.

DID YOU KNOW?
Mythical griffins may have arisen from the discovery of the dinosaur Protoceratops' fossils.

8 Next add two large, curved wings. Rub out any mistakes if you need to – this step is tricky!

9 Draw the details below to complete the griffin's feathery wings.

10 Add the tail next – make it long and thin with a tuft on the end like a lion's tail.

11 Rub out any guide lines, then bring your griffin to life with coloured pens, pencils or crayons.

GORGONS

Gorgons appear among the **oldest** mythical monsters on record, featuring in ancient Greek art and said to guard the gates of the Underworld. The most famous gorgons were Sthenno, Euryale and Medusa, three **terrifying snake-haired sisters**.

APPEARANCE: snakes for hair, bulging eyes, sometimes described as horrifying while others told of the gorgons' beauty

ORIGIN: ancient Greece

ALSO KNOWN AS: sea demons

STRENGTHS: Medusa could turn anyone who looked upon her gaze to stone. Sthenno and Euryale were immortal, while Medusa was not

WEAKNESSES: Medusa fell to the sword of Perseus, who chopped off the gorgon's head

DANGER RATING: 💀💀💀
Positively petrifying!

FIVE THINGS YOU SHOULD KNOW ABOUT GORGONS

5 The three gorgon sisters were the monstrous daughters of the sea gods Phorcys and Ceto.

4 Legends tell that gorgons' blood was poisonous, with drops of blood forming venomous snakes from Africa.

3 The warrior Perseus used Medusa's severed head as a weapon, as it continued to turn onlookers into stone.

2 Both Zeus and Athena were said to bear the symbol of Medusa's head on their armour.

1 The gorgons were sometimes described as having wings – flight making them even more dangerous!

MONSTER DISCOVERY

Reveal the name of this chilling creature from Puerto Rico by circling every second letter on the path.

DID YOU KNOW?
The monster's name translates from the Spanish as 'goat-sucker', as the beast is said to suck the blood of goats, sheep and other farm animals.

START:
L
L
I
H
P
U
R
P
A
C
M
A
S
H
A
O
B
T
R
E
A

DID YOU KNOW?
The earliest sightings of the creature were only reported as recently as 1995, and may have been influenced by horror film creations.

Now you know the name of the mystery monster, imagine that you had travelled to Latin America to track down the beast. File a report with as much detail about the creatures as you can.

Pawprint:

Droppings:

Image:

Danger rating:

THE KRAKEN

A **terrifying tentacled beast** that has long troubled sailors in the seas of Northern Europe. Reports of the mighty Kraken may not have been fiction, although these were likely sightings of **giant squid**.

APPEARANCE: an enormous squid-like beast, with powerful, suckered tentacles and haunting black eyes

ORIGIN: the North Atlantic Ocean between Norway and Iceland

ALSO KNOWN AS: sea-mischief, giant squid

STRENGTHS: can pull large ships beneath the waves in a swoop of its tentacles

WEAKNESSES: unable to survive out of water

DANGER RATING:

A sailor's worst nightmare!

FIVE THINGS YOU SHOULD KNOW ABOUT THE KRAKEN

5 The Kraken was first described in the 13th century Norse saga *Örvar-Oddr*, where the hero Oddr is said to have defeated the legendary beast.

4 The beast is said to inhabit the seas where underwater volcanoes are found – including the bubbling waters and strong currents around Iceland and Greece.

3 While these days we think of the Kraken looking like a giant squid, early reports of the sea-beast describe it as having crab-like legs.

2 It may be a curious creature, but the Kraken possesses no magical or supernatural abilities, unlike some other mythical monsters.

1 It is said to be a solitary beast, spending its days scouring the seabed for prey, while surfacing only occasionally if disturbed.

POTION-MAKING

Choose your own quantities from the mythical ingredients below to brew a perilous potion! Decide what you would want the potion to do and who might drink it.

QUANTITY:

.... phoenix tears
.... unicorn tail-hair
.... vampire fang
.... werewolf fur
.... dragon egg
.... zombie drool
.... bunyip poop (be sure to wear gloves!)
.... Kraken's tentacle
.... basilisk blood
.... mermaid scales
.... fairy dust
.... Minotaur horn
.... ogre bogeys
.... goblin toenails

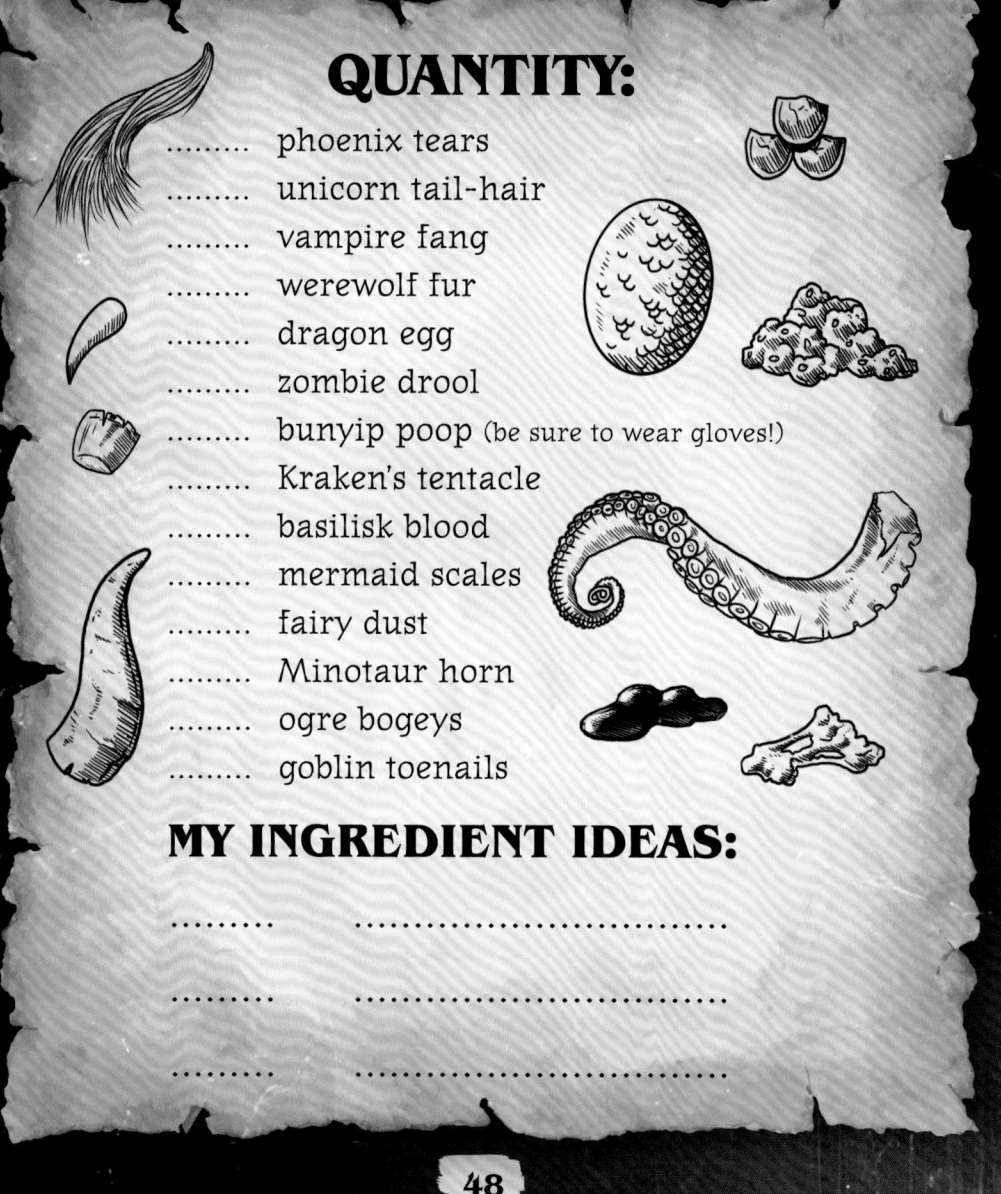

MY INGREDIENT IDEAS:

....

....

....

What would the purpose of the spell be?

....

....

Who or what would you use the potion on?

....

....

THE LOCH NESS MONSTER

A large lake in the Scottish Highlands is reportedly home to a **huge aquatic animal** known as the Loch Ness Monster. In Scottish folklore, a long-necked beast has lived in the loch for at least 1,500 years.

APPEARANCE: a large humped creature with a long neck and flippers

ORIGIN: Loch Ness, Scotland

ALSO KNOWN AS: Nessie, the Beast of Loch Ness

STRENGTHS: camouflage – Nessie largely remains undetected in the murky waters of the loch

WEAKNESSES: the monster is confined to live in Loch Ness

DANGER RATING: **Not a threat to humans**

FIVE THINGS YOU SHOULD KNOW ABOUT THE LOCH NESS MONSTER

5 Some sightings of the monster – such as upturned boats or wave patterns on the water – could be explained away as optical illusions.

4 In 1933, tracks were found of an unidentified animal close to the shores of the loch. The tracks were later revealed to have been faked, using a stuffed hippopotamus foot.

3 During World War II in 1941, an Italian newspaper reported that its nation's army bombed the Scottish loch and with it the famous monster.

2 Many believe that the creature could be a plesiosaur, a marine reptile believed to have gone extinct about 65.5 million years ago.

1 Of the hundreds of thousands of tourists and monster-hunters that visit Loch Ness each year, not one has managed to prove that Nessie really does exist.

NIGHTMARE!

Dreams can sometimes be scary and random, and even cause us to wake up in a cold sweat – nightmare! But dig a little deeper and those dreams about monsters might just have a hidden meaning. Here's how to interpret three ghoulish dreams...

VAMPIRE

A vampire creeping into your dream can indicate that you are worried about something that is beyond your control – leaving you, the dreamer, feeling anxious or lost. A tough challenge may be heading your way, so keep friends and loved ones close by. Problems never seem quite as scary when shared with those you trust.

WEREWOLF

A dream about a werewolf could be alerting you that something or someone around you is not what it seems – take a step back while you investigate. If your dream was about turning into a werewolf, it may mean that you are losing sight of who you really are. Perhaps you are putting too much energy into friendships or activities that you no longer enjoy, or you have a bad habit that needs breaking? Time for a change, perhaps?

MERMAID

If a mermaid has splashed into your dreams, it could mean that a change or a bigger transformation is about to take place. If the chance to try something new in the next weeks and months does come your way, be curious and trust your instincts – it could prove more magical than monstrous!

Now fill in your own dream diary as soon as you wake up each morning, for a whole week. Did any mythical monsters make an appearance? Record everything you can remember, including how you felt.

Night 1 ....
....

Night 2 ....
....

Night 3 ....
....

Night 4 ....
....

Night 5 ....
....

Night 6 ....
....

Night 7 ....
....

MERMAIDS

Spirits of the sea, mermaids lured sailors to their death with their **sweet singing voices**, causing them to crash their ships on **rocky shores**. These curious creatures combined the head and upper body of a human with the tail of a fish.

APPEARANCE: long-haired beauties with a human upper body and a fish's tail

ORIGIN: ancient Greece and Rome

ALSO KNOWN AS: sirens (mistakenly), merfolk or merpeople. A male mermaid is called a merman

STRENGTHS: able to live and breathe underwater, can hypnotize with their song

WEAKNESSES: cannot survive on land

DANGER RATING:  **Beautiful but deadly!**

FIVE THINGS YOU SHOULD KNOW ABOUT MERMAIDS

5 Mermaids are sometimes confused with sirens, but they are not the same creature; sirens have the body and wings of a bird, in place of a fish tail.

4 The fearsome pirate captain Blackbeard was rumoured to be terrified of mermaids and steered his ship well away from seas in which the creatures might dwell.

3 The famous explorer Christopher Columbus once mistook a manatee for a mermaid and was disappointed that it wasn't as beautiful as he'd imagined!

2 Scottish shape-shifters known as selkie share a connection with mermaids, though they have the added ability of being able to transform into human form while on land.

1 Some scientists, including Charles Darwin, believed that humans evolved from mermaids.

WOULD YOU RATHER?

Let your imagination transport you to a place where monsters are more than myth... Answer the following questions pretending that the beasts below roam freely among us. Choose your answers wisely!

1 Battle an angry ogre or a beastly basilisk?
☐ ogre ☐ basilisk

2 Swim the seas with a mermaid or the Kraken?
☐ mermaid ☐ Kraken

3 Race an undead zombie or a galloping unicorn?
☐ zombie ☐ unicorn

4 Invite a hungry bunyip or a thirsty vampire to dinner?
☐ bunyip ☐ vampire

5 Take to the skies on a fiery phoenix or a golden griffin?
☐ phoenix ☐ griffin

6 Be able to breathe fire like a dragon or turn people to stone like a gorgon?
☐ fire-breathing ☐ stone-turning

7 Hire a goblin to do your housework or a fairy to do your homework?
☐ goblin ☐ fairy

8 Have a magical unicorn or a pretty phoenix as a pet?
☐ unicorn ☐ phoenix

9 Grow a serpent's tail or have hair made from snakes?

☐ tail ☐ hair

10 Have the ability to howl like a werewolf or sing as sweetly as a mermaid?

☐ werewolf ☐ mermaid

11 Give the yeti a haircut or a zombie a makeover?

☐ yeti ☐ zombie

12 Have a unicorn's horn or a mermaid's tail?

☐ unicorn horn ☐ mermaid tail

Now think of some more strange scenarios choosing between mythical monsters…

13
....
....
☐ .... ☐ ....

14
....
....
☐ .... ☐ ....

THE MINOTAUR

According to Greek mythology, the Minotaur was a monster with the body of a man and the **head and tail of a bull**, the only one of his kind. The creature guarded the Labyrinth built for King Minos of Crete, a **complex maze** from which it was said to be impossible to escape.

APPEARANCE: with its savage bull's head and muscly body, many considered the Minotaur to be a fierce beast

ORIGIN: the island of Crete, ancient Greece

ALSO KNOWN AS: Asterion, meaning 'starry one'

STRENGTHS: superhuman power, horns that could demolish walls

WEAKNESSES: not the most intelligent creature, heavy and slow

DANGER RATING:

Outwitted and defeated by Theseus

FIVE THINGS YOU SHOULD KNOW ABOUT THE MINOTAUR

5 With the help of Ariadne, Theseus killed the Minotaur before exiting the maze by following a line of thread he had laid in a trail.

4 Some saw the Minotaur as a gentle and misunderstood creature, unfairly banished to the Labyrinth because of his ferocious appearance.

3 The Minotaur could uproot a tree with his powerful horns.

2 Some stories tell of the Minotaur being able to breathe fire.

1 Although the Minotaur was half-bull, he was definitely carnivorous and was said to feast on human flesh.

SPOOKY CELEBRATION

There's no need to wait until Halloween to host a spooky party – you can have a fang-tastic celebration at any time of the year! Choose a date and time, then get planning your monster bash.

FOOD
- ☐ monster eyeball cookies
- ☐ ghostly s'mores
- ☐ werewolf hot dogs
- ☐ mummy meatballs
- ☐ zombie-brain popcorn
- ☐ garlic dough-(eye)balls

other ideas:

DRINKS
- ☐ beastly berry smoothie
- ☐ rotten-apple slushy
- ☐ zombie brew
- ☐ blood-orange fizz
- ☐ fairy float

other ideas:

COSTUMES
- ☐ werewolf
- ☐ mermaid
- ☐ zombie
- ☐ vampire
- ☐ yeti
- ☐ ogre
- ☐ fairy
- ☐ faun

other ideas:

PROPS
- ☐ fairy lights
- ☐ creepy netting
- ☐ fake spider's webs
- ☐ glow-sticks
- ☐ garlic garlands

other ideas:

Now to choose a playlist to get the party started. Which spooky songs will get your friends on the dance floor? Decide your top ten songs below.

FLOOR FILLERS

1 Artist:........................ Song:........................

2 Artist:........................ Song:........................

3 Artist:........................ Song:........................

4 Artist:........................ Song:........................

5 Artist:........................ Song:........................

6 Artist:........................ Song:........................

7 Artist:........................ Song:........................

8 Artist:........................ Song:........................

9 Artist:........................ Song:........................

10 Artist:........................ Song:........................

OGRES

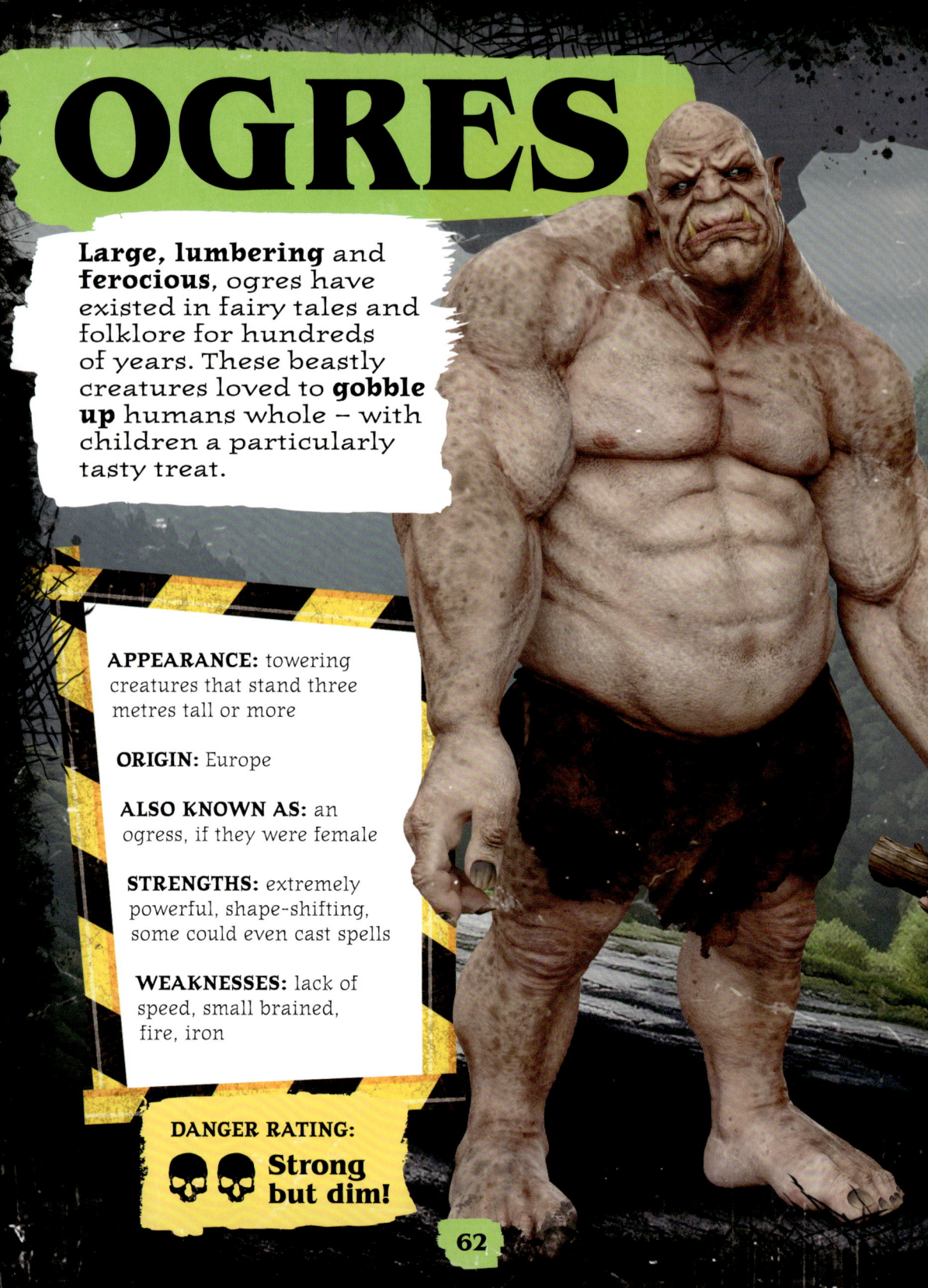

Large, lumbering and **ferocious**, ogres have existed in fairy tales and folklore for hundreds of years. These beastly creatures loved to **gobble up** humans whole – with children a particularly tasty treat.

APPEARANCE: towering creatures that stand three metres tall or more

ORIGIN: Europe

ALSO KNOWN AS: an ogress, if they were female

STRENGTHS: extremely powerful, shape-shifting, some could even cast spells

WEAKNESSES: lack of speed, small brained, fire, iron

DANGER RATING: 💀💀 **Strong but dim!**

FIVE THINGS YOU SHOULD KNOW ABOUT OGRES

5 Size-wise, ogres are bigger than trolls but smaller than giants.

4 You might find an ogre living in a forest or a mountain cave, while others call castles their home.

3 Some scientists believe that ogres may have been Neanderthals, an extinct human species that once lived in Europe and parts of Asia.

2 Ogres are usually illustrated wearing little clothing, often just a loincloth made from animal skin.

1 Ogres are said to be fearful of fire, while weapons made from iron can also defeat them.

FRIGHT NIGHT

Plan a creepy sleepover for you and your bravest mates, then prepare to be scared! Mix up your top ten scary movies, TV shows and video games, and start the countdown to the beastly binge. Pick out clips or choose spooky games to play, then vote on the scare factor for each.

10
Name:
Monsters:
Scare factor: 💀💀💀💀💀

! WARNING! Watching scary shows may leave you unable to sleep!

9
Name:
Monsters:
Scare factor: 💀💀💀💀💀

8
Name:
Monsters:
Scare factor: 💀💀💀💀💀

7
Name:
Monsters:
Scare factor: 💀💀💀💀💀

PHOENIXES

Said to live for more than **500 years**, the majestic phoenix sets itself alight and is **consumed by fire** at the end of its life. From the ashes, a new bird rises, symbolising the cycle of death and rebirth.

APPEARANCE: stunning fiery feathers, with plumes of red, orange and gold

ORIGIN: ancient Rome and Greece, now appears in myths worldwide

ALSO KNOWN AS: Bennu (Egypt), Fènghuáng (China)

ABILITIES: each phoenix can rise from its own ashes

WEAKNESSES: although the phoenix is immortal, iron weapons can cause it damage

DANGER RATING:
 More healing than harmful to humans

FIVE THINGS YOU SHOULD KNOW ABOUT PHOENIXES

5 The tears of a phoenix can magically heal many human injuries and illnesses.

4 In Egyptian mythology, the phoenix is known as the Bennu bird, which has the appearance of a stork or heron-like bird.

3 The nest the phoenix builds when it senses death is close is made out of twigs from sweet-smelling myrrh and cinnamon trees.

2 Greek legend tells of the phoenix's beautiful songs attracting the sun god Apollo, who stopped his chariot to listen each day.

1 In the present day, an unlikely comeback is described as being 'like a phoenix'.

MONSTER MOVES

Level up your usual exercise routine with these fast-paced monster activities, designed to get you moving monster style.

WEREWOLF WARM-UP

💀 To sprint at supernatural speed like a werewolf, first you'll need to warm up.

💀 Make a small obstacle course to get your muscles moving – gather small toys, empty boxes or even pairs of socks, then lay them out three paces apart.

💀 Race through the obstacles without touching them as quickly as you can.

💀 Friends should howl loudly if any obstacles are accidentally touched!

💀 You could even dribble a ball around the obstacles.

ZOMBIE WALK

A game for three or more players

☠ Pick one person to be the zombie slayer. They should face a wall, with their back to the others.

☠ The remaining players are zombies and should line up ten steps away.

☠ While the slayer's back is turned, the zombies must move forward.

☠ The slayer can turn around at any moment and shout 'Freeze!' – any zombie caught moving must return to the start.

☠ If a zombie touches the slayer, the game ends, and you swap roles.

MERMAID STRIKE

A game for three or more players

☠ Choose one person to be the mermaid, while the others are sailors.

☠ When the mermaid starts to sing, the sailors must take refuge out of the ocean (off the floor).

☠ The last person to find dry land is out.

☠ When all the sailors are out, swap roles so there's a new menacing mermaid.

UNICORNS

Beautiful and **shy**, Unicorns are the least monstrous of the mythical creatures in this book but they are no less legendary. Traditionally white, a single spiralled horn on the unicorn's head was said to be able to **magically heal** wounds as well as heartbreak.

APPEARANCE: a pony-like creature with a magical horn on its head

ORIGIN: unicorns have appeared in myths and legends all over the world for more than 6,000 years

ALSO KNOWN AS: alicorns (unicorns with wings) and mermicorns (mermaid-like unicorns)

ABILITIES: healing, flight (alicorns), can swim (mermicorns)

WEAKNESSES: lions are the natural enemy of the unicorn

DANGER RATING:
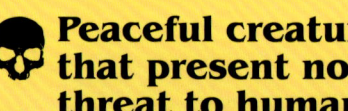 **Peaceful creatures that present no threat to humans**

FIVE THINGS YOU SHOULD KNOW ABOUT UNICORNS

5 The name 'unicorn' means 'one horn' and originates from ancient Latin.

4 Shy creatures, unicorns live in small herds called blessings.

3 The qilin or kirin appears in ancient Chinese mythology – a single-horned creature that is part dragon, part lion.

2 A drawing of a unicorn was discovered in the Lascaux Caves of southwestern France, dating back as far as 15,000 BCE.

1 Unicorn horns were prized by kings and queens centuries ago, with Queen Elizabeth I and Russian ruler Ivan the Terrible each presented with a magical horn.

GHOULS GALLERY

Grab your pens and get set to draw a gruesome gallery of mythical monsters. Read the descriptions, then fill each frame with a beast that fits. Finally, decide on the scare factor for each freaky creation.

Dream up a deadly dragon.

Design a howling werewolf.

SCARE FACTOR

Invent a venomous basilisk.

SCARE FACTOR

SCARE FACTOR

VAMPIRES

Monsters in human form, these legendary creatures remain **undead** by feasting on fresh human blood. It is rumoured that when a vampire bites its victim, usually on the neck, a second vampire is born. While difficult to defeat, there are plenty of tactics to try.

APPEARANCE: pale, sun-deprived skin, fanged teeth, long fingernails

ORIGIN: Eastern Europe

ALSO KNOWN AS: vampyres, ekimmu

STRENGTHS: shape-shifting, eyes can change colour

WEAKNESSES: mirrors, garlic, sunlight, stake through the heart, holy crosses and holy water

DANGER RATING:

Can be overcome multiple ways

FIVE THINGS YOU SHOULD KNOW ABOUT VAMPIRES

5 Vampires cannot see their reflection in a mirror as the mirror's silver lining causes the image to dissolve.

4 The Transylvanian count Dracula is the most infamous vampire in history and appeared in Bram Stoker's novel, first published in 1897.

3 Vampires are believed to have been real, with reports of blood-sucking humans dating back to ancient Babylon, some four thousand years ago.

2 A heavy stone monument called a dolmen is often placed over the grave of a suspected vampire to prevent its evil spirit from escaping.

1 Brides wore garlic under their wedding dresses, while sailors took bulbs of the smelly stuff to sea to protect against a vampire attack.

HOW TO AVOID A VAMPIRE ENCOUNTER

While meetings with these creatures of the night remain pretty rare, here are some tips to keep villainous vampires away and how to survive an unfortunate encounter.

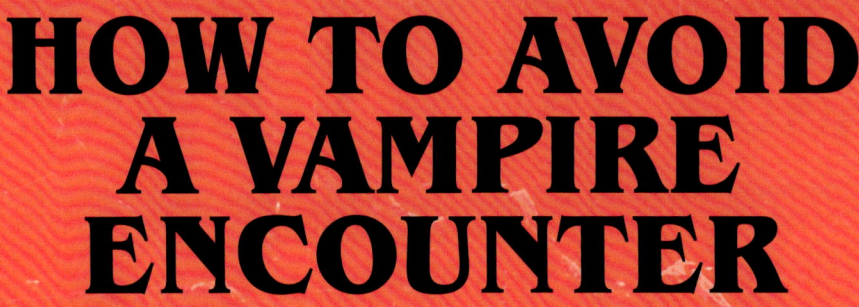

Wear a necklace of garlic or carry a bulb in a bag. A garland of garlic on your front door can also deter the blood-sucking fiends from entering.

Vampires can't stand sunlight and sleep the day away in their coffin, emerging at night in search of fresh flesh. You'll be safe outside during daylight hours, but be sure to head home before the sun sets.

Wearing a crucifix or holy cross is said to be another way to repel these powerful demons.

Similarly, holy water can be used in an encounter with a vampire, causing the demon's skin to burn and scar.

Some shape-shifting vampires, including Count Dracula himself, can turn into bats. Patch up any holes in your home, where bats could squeeze through.

To get rid of a vampire for good, a wooden stake driven through its heart should do the trick. It is said that the stake must be made from the wood of an ash tree.

Never look a vampire directly in the eye, if you want to avoid falling for its charms.

Scattering a packet of seeds around you can slow down a vampire – they're compelled to stop and pick up the seeds. Then make a swift exit!

WEREWOLVES

Steer clear of these **shape-shifters** on a dark night or you might end up on the menu! These chilling creatures appear as normal humans by day, suddenly sprouting fur and transforming into **howling wolves** at night. Werewolves are at their most fearsome under a full moon.

APPEARANCE: human by day, usually grey or dark fur and glowing eyes by night

ORIGIN: ancient Babylon, Greece and Rome

ALSO KNOWN AS: lycanthropes (from the Greek words for 'wolf' and 'human')

STRENGTHS: shape-shifting, night vision, speed and power

WEAKNESSES: silver bullets and weapons made from silver, mercury, wolfsbane (a small blue flower)

DANGER RATING: 💀💀💀 **Howling horrors**

FIVE THINGS YOU SHOULD KNOW ABOUT WEREWOLVES

5 Some say that you can only become a werewolf after receiving a bite from the fabled furry fiend, while others believe that werewolf genes can be passed down through the generations.

4 Once bitten, the 'werewolf's curse' cannot be reversed.

3 Holy water offers little protection against werewolves, while sprinkling salt outside your home does ward off the creatures.

2 Werewolves can heal themselves of injuries without the need for modern medicine.

1 Werewolves share a pack mentality. If one of the pack feels pain or passes away, the others can feel it too.

FACT OR FOLKLORE?

Some animals are so bizarre it would be easy to believe that they didn't actually exist! Can you work out which creatures below are the real deal and which only appear in folklore? Make your way through the maze landing only on the beasts that are definitely mythical.

START

narwhal	megalodon	blobfish	griffin
okapi	bird of paradise	bearded dragon	bunyip
platypus	rhinoceros	yeti	vampire deer
golden lion tamarin	Medusa	Matamata turtle	axolotl
giant squid	cyclopes	Tasmanian devil	ghost shark

FINISH

Now find the names of twenty totally mythical monsters in the word grid below. Their names may read forwards, backwards, up, down and diagonally.

BASILISK
BUNYIP
CERBERUS
CYCLOPES
DRAGON

FAIRY
GORGON
GRIFFIN
KRAKEN
LOCH NESS MONSTER

MERMAID
MINOTAUR
OGRE
PHOENIX
TROLL

UNICORN
VAMPIRE
WEREWOLF
YETI
ZOMBIE

```
            S P
          U C G F
        R J N L X G
      E S I O I R O R
    B P S W N C T B Y I
  R V Y E E T E Y R I A F
E I W R O P N N E K A R K F
C T N E H C G D R A G O N U Q I
F E R W P D I A M R E M B N D S L N
P Y R E T S N O M S S E N H C O L M V P
K I G M I N O T A U R W N T F O T F V U
  V Y K A W N R O C I N U S R L L A U
    Y N M I S W O W E Y G T I G M N
      G U U L G O R G O N X H P E
        E B S E P O L C Y C I U
          B A S I L I S K R W
            A Z O M B I E O
              T V Q S B G
                T D P R
                  F E
```

THE YETI

In the **snow-capped mountains** of the Himalayas, tales of a huge roaming **beast** have been shared by locals and explorers for centuries.

APPEARANCE: two to three metres tall, ape-like, thick fur, large feet

ORIGIN: the Himalayas – Bhutan, China, India, Nepal, Siberia

ALSO KNOWN AS: the Abominable Snowman

STRENGTHS: an expert at camouflage, adapted to survive in extreme temperatures and at high altitudes

WEAKNESSES: moves slowly

DANGER RATING: 💀💀💀
Best avoided!

FIVE THINGS YOU SHOULD KNOW ABOUT THE YETI

5 Sightings of the yeti have told of a creature that walked on two legs, with descriptions of its fur varying reddish-brown to polar white.

4 The word 'yeti' comes from the Tibetan word 'yeh-teh', which means 'man-like animal'.

3 Possible yeti footprints were reported as far back as 1899 by Scottish explorer Laurence Waddell, while exploring Mount Everest.

2 Hair samples said to belong to the yeti have been proved to come from more common creatures such as bears, cows and raccoons in DNA tests.

1 Meanwhile, a monastery in Nepal was home to a finger long believed to belong to the yeti. Tests later proved it was in fact a human finger!

IN SEARCH OF MONSTERS

Are you brave enough to go hunting for monsters? Plan out an epic trip below.

WHERE WILL YOU TRAVEL?

Europe ☐
North America ☐
South America ☐
Africa ☐
Asia ☐
Australia ☐
Antarctica ☐

HOW WILL YOU GET THERE?

walk ☐
car ☐
bus/coach ☐
train ☐
plane ☐
boat ☐

my choice: ....

WHO WILL YOU TRAVEL WITH?

I'll go solo ☐
my best friend ☐
a family member ☐
somebody else:

HOW WILL YOU PROVE THAT THE CREATURE EXISTS?

sketches ☐
photos ☐
videos ☐
voice recordings ☐
footprint moulds ☐

samples of:
eggshell ☐
bone ☐
poop ☐

other evidence:

WHO WOULD YOU SHARE YOUR FINDINGS WITH?

I'd keep them secret and leave the beast in peace ☐
only my closest friends and family members ☐
I'd create some social media videos ☐
The press – newspaper and TV reporters ☐

somebody else:

ZOMBIES

Zombies are humans that have been brought back from the dead, often through **dark magic**. People can also join the walking dead after being **infected** by an undeadly virus or suffering a zombie bite. The idea of zombies is older than you might think – the ancient Greeks weighed down skeletons in graves with rocks to stop the dead from rising.

APPEARANCE: pale or greenish skin, flesh may have begun to rot

ORIGIN: Haiti, a Caribbean nation

ALSO KNOWN AS: ghouls, flesh-eaters, the living dead

ABILITIES: can survive being attacked with weapons, some zombies are lightning-fast

WEAKNESSES: easy to outwit, many zombies can only shuffle slowly

DANGER RATING:

Most dangerous when in packs

FIVE THINGS YOU SHOULD KNOW ABOUT ZOMBIES

5 The word zombie is thought to have come from the Kongo word 'nzambi' meaning 'god'.

4 Feeding a zombie salt is said to make it return to its grave, where it goes back to being dead.

3 According to folklore, the only way to defeat a zombie is to destroy its brain.

2 Not all zombies were once human – animals such as dogs and cats can join the undead too!

1 Avoid getting too close to a zombie at all costs – if one manages to bite you, you'll become infected too.

HOW TO SURVIVE A ZOMBIE APOCALYPSE

Now you've got the lowdown on these deadly creepers, here's what to do if zombies ever try to invade your neighbourhood. Read on to improve your chances of survival!

PACK SUPPLIES

- ☐ tinned and dried food
- ☐ pet food
- ☐ can-opener
- ☐ torch
- ☐ batteries and chargers
- ☐ medical kit
- ☐ sleeping bag
- ☐ small tent
- ☐ phone or GPS device
- ☐ matches or fire-lighting kit
- ☐ portable radio
- ☐ cash
- ☐ toilet roll
- ☐ shower gel
- ☐ toothbrush and toothpaste

MY OWN IDEAS: ....

....

....

TEAM UP

Work out who's good in a crisis – who's good at fixing things, who could help nurse you back to health and which green-fingered friend can grow their own food. Choose your friends wisely – each member of the team should bring a valuable skill.

BRING THE DOG!

With their keen sense of smell, dogs can alert you to the whiff of zombie danger before it's too late. Train your pet not to bark too loudly and give away your hiding place.

LEAVE TOWN
The next thing to do is to get out of the city, where infected zombies will spread the virus more easily. Head to the countryside and find shelter, ideally close to a freshwater source like a stream or a reservoir.

SET UP A BASE
If you've managed to find shelter indoors, use all available locks, board up windows and draw down blackout blinds – zombies aren't the brightest and are likely to move on if they think no one's home.

DON'T DRINK THE WATER
As the virus spreads, water sources can quickly become contaminated. Boil water to kill any bugs and filter any cloudy water through a paper towel into a plastic water bottle, then use the sun's UV rays to disinfect the water.

STAY POSITIVE
It could take weeks to sit out the storm, so keep everyone's spirits up with games and of course the odd joke. Here's one to get you started … Why did the zombie stay off school? It felt rotten!

GOOD LUCK OUT THERE, PEOPLE!

WHICH MYTHICAL MONSTER ARE YOU?

No two people are the same, as every mythical creature is different. Answer the questions truthfully to discover which **mythical monster** is the closest match to your personality.

What's more important to you?
- Being true to yourself.
- Making others happy.

What would your special ability be?
- Flight – you love soaring the skies!
- Extraordinary strength.

What are you naturally drawn to?
- Gold or treasure – at the end of a rainbow.
- Beautiful things from the natural world – the ocean, the moon and starry skies.

When do you have the most fun?
- I love delving into the pages a book or solving a puzzle. → **DRAGON** Bold and intelligent, you're not afraid to accept new challenges.
- When I'm hanging out with family or friends. → **GRIFFIN** Lion-hearted and loyal, you'd make a great griffin.

How do you tackle a tricky piece of homework?
- You use your creativity to solve the problem project. → **PHOENIX** Imaginative and bold, a phoenix is your perfect match.
- You leave it to the last minute and get others to help you out. → **FAIRY** Lively and fun, you sprinkle a little magic everywhere you go

How often do you squabble with friends or family?
- Hardly ever. Any squabbles magically never last long. → **UNICORN** One of a kind, you love to explore magical places.
- My temper sometimes causes arguments! → **OGRE** You love to be the centre of attention and are not afraid to make yourself heard!

Would you rather live on land or under the sea?
- Under the sea where I'm mostly left in peace. → **KRAKEN** Cool and curious, you hold more power than you might think!
- On land where you can roam freely under the light of the moon. → **WEREWOLF** Athletic and strong, you feel most energetic at night.

ANSWERS

Pages 12-13
MYTH BUSTING

The Sphinx's riddle: a human – who crawls on all fours as an infant, walks on two legs when grown and uses a walking stick in old age.

1. dragon
2. phoenix
3. vampire
4. mermaid
5. werewolf
6. zombie
7. unicorn
8. Loch Ness Monster

Pages 32–33
MONSTER MASH

1. OGRE, 2. MERMAID, 3. ZOMBIE, 4. WEREWOLF, 5. GRIFFIN, 6. GOBLIN, 7. DRAGON, 8. KRAKEN, 9. BASILISK, 10. Vampire, 11. YETI, 12. PHOENIX.

Page 44
MONSTER DISCOVERY

CHUPACABRA

Pages 80–81
FACT OR FOLKLORE?

START

narwhal — megalodon — blobfish — griffin

okapi — bird of paradise — bearded dragon — bunyip

platypus — rhinoceros — yeti — vampire deer

golden lion tamarin — Medusa — Matamata turtle — axolotl

giant squid — cyclopes — Tasmanian devil — ghost shark

FINISH